Cool Hair

PICTURES & WORDS
BY DASHEEMA JARRETT-JONES

Cool Hair

IAMORJ

Print ISBN: 978-0-578-88737-1

Printed in the United States of America

Dedication

Thank you Jesus for your love, words, and vision for Cool Hair.

This book is dedicated to my loving momma Mary, who never missed a beat to style her grandson's hair while caring for us during a pandemic. Thank you for your tender love and care.

To my husband Ishaaq (Izzy), mommas Mary, Sylvia, Donna and cousin Raye, thank you for your inspiration and editorial insight. I love you all gingerly.

To my son Israel, nieces, nephews, and baby readers you are beautiful. I love you and Jesus loves you and your cool hair!

This Book Belongs to Cool Hair:

_____

Date:

_____

Hey, hey, before we play, what new cool hairstyle will Granny do today?

Of course it's a surprise, six parts with twist and small rubber band ties.

Hey, hey, it's wash day. Can you guess what Granny will do to my hair today?

Oh yay! Combing next. Three cool twist, and she slicks down rest.

A cute little bun she pulls up for fun.

Oh, here she goes!
Time for my favorite
braided cornrows.

Today she washes my hair clean, adds conditioner and tells me I am a King.

Now it's time for a photo of my beautiful curly finger coils.

I love my cool hair everywhere.

Granny plays with her dreads on my head.

Afro day to let my hair rest before I play.

My Granny loves me so much. She shows it in every cool hairstyle. Granny always makes me smile.

I love my Granny and she loves me too.

Always remember God loves you for you!

What is your favorite cool hairdo on you? I love my hair and the creative things my Granny can do!

Here's some hair patterns you can try too!

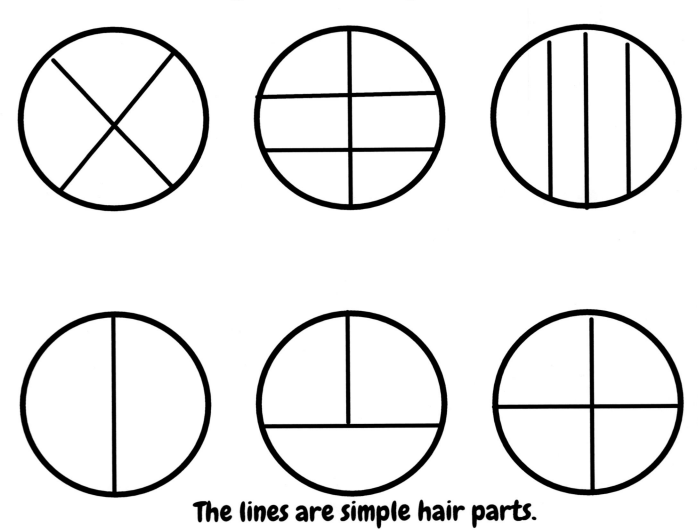

The lines are simple hair parts.

Maybe there's a cool hairdo for you. Use these circles and see what you can do!

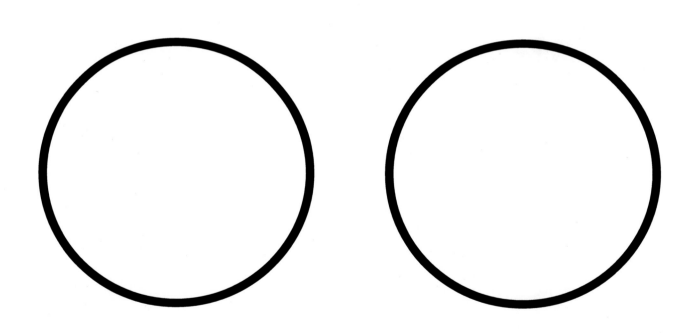

Date:_____

Don't stop there! When you get bigger, draw each family member's cool hair!

Date:_____

Made in the USA
Monee, IL
15 May 2023

33185319R00021